Good Business Sense for Doing Good Business

Good Business Sense for Doing Good Business

A Guide to Enhance Your Business Acumen

Donald C. Yates Ed.D.

To order additional copies of this book, contact:
Xlibris
844-714-8691
www.Xlibris.com
Orders@Xlibris.com
823198

CONTENTS

WRITING

CULTURAL AWARENESS

Preface

In the world of work, there are many facets which combine to form a true business persona – an image that you, a businessman, wish to project to any with whom you will interact. Through an understanding of the following series of articles and other commentary depicted here regarding the process and product of company interaction, you will be able to understand more fully your duties and obligations within your sphere of influence and emerge as a leader and an influencer of business.

After two introductory articles regarding *leadership* and its true essence, you will learn about the ways that *interactivity* skills can bolster your work efforts and result in better *productivity*, both for yourself as well as your company and its aims. It is how you are able to merge with your company's goals that will create your direction and advancement "up the corporate ladder."

You will then be made aware of the nature of *language* and its impact within your self-expression. Word usage and punctuation are stressed here in order for you to be more precise in both oral and written presentations and be more accurate with what you want to say and how you want to say it.

Once you understand the essentials of language acuity, you will learn about the process of *writing* and its crucial impact on your audience as you move from your receptive skills of reading and listening to the use of your expressive skills of writing and speaking. Styles of written expression are presented as well as information about the art of decision-making as it relates to what you write and say in your everyday activities.

In the final section, you will see two articles focused upon how well you know your audience as you present yourself. You will learn that *cultural awareness* underlies all aspects of your work, and your knowledge of whom you need to reach and how you actually reach them leads to your personal research and development towards your recipients.

An understanding of the five sections presented will result in ways to approach your work and, in fact, may give you insights into areas you need to address to be that much more attuned to the higher levels of involvement to which you aspire. Use each of these suggestive ideas and scenarios as you wish, and you will be pleasantly surprised.

Don Yates

The Traits of Leadership

What qualities do leaders have that the rest of us do not have, queries John W. Gardner, noted Professor in the Graduate School of Business at Stanford University. He states that there are no traits that will guarantee successful leadership in all situations as leadership is not absolutely "situation specific." However, the probability is greater than chance that leaders in one situation will be leaders in another situation.

Gardner presents a series of fourteen attributes which may not appear in every leader but are seen in every leader who is effective, depending upon a given situation:

1. *Physical Vitality and Stamina* – Physical presence and command posture as well as long-term involvement with a situation is crucial.

2. *Intelligence and "Judgement-in Action"* – Judgement is the ability to combine hard data, questionable data, and intuitive guesses to arrive at a conclusion that, in situations, proves to be correct. Judgement-in-action includes effective problem solving, the design of strategies, the setting of priorities, and intuitive as well as rational judgements. Most important, these qualities include the capacity to appraise the potentialities of co-workers and, of course, of opponents.

3. *Willingness and Eagerness to Accept Responsibility* – The aptitude to embrace aspects of change and direction and to

do so unhesitatingly creates an atmosphere of ownership and involvement.

4. *Task Competence* – Top-level leaders cannot hope to have competency in more than a few of the matters under their jurisdiction, but they must have knowledge of the whole system that they oversee, as well as its mission, and be aware of the environment in which it functions.

5. *Understanding of Followers/Constituents and Their Needs* – To know that those who work with you and under you have wants and desires which they need to have met is to be conscious of the vitality of the whole which will insure the direction to be taken.

6. *Skill in Dealing with People* – The ability to "read" peoples' wants and needs along with how those needs mesh with the aims and goals of the company is an essential trait of leadership.

7. *Capacity to Motivate* – More than any other attribute, this skill is close to the heart of the popular consensus of leadership – the capacity to move people to action, to communicate persuasively, and to strengthen the confidence of followers.

8. *Need to Achieve* – A true leader must have a strong desire to see and feel the aims and goals to which he/she aspires.

9. *Courage, Resolution, Steadiness* - Clearly, a leader needs courage – not just bravery of the moment but courage over time, not just willingness to risk but to risk again and again, to function well under prolonged stress, to survive defeat and keep going.

10. *Capacity to Win and Hold Trust* - A leader can oftentimes see the finish line of a project before others can and, therefore, use that forward vision to captivate and motivate others to strive harder.

11. *Capacity to Manage, Decide, and Set Priorities* – Organization and purposeful direction are sound qualities of leadership. Managing time and tasks, deciding both short-term and long-term courses of action, and an ongoing reevaluating of these processes allow the leader to be involved in the best practices of work activity.

12. *Confidence* – Confidence is an essential trait to motivate the risks that leaders take. It takes confidence to handle the criticism and hostility that leaders must absorb.

13. *Ascendence, Dominance, and Assertiveness* - The individuals who achieve in leadership roles are apt to have a fairly strong impulse to take charge. Their assertiveness doesn't necessarily conform to the stereotype of the visibly forceful leader – some are quiet and unspectacular – but whatever their outward style, their inner impulse is to leave their thumbprint on events.

14. *Adaptability, Flexibility of Approach* – Being able to adjust an approach as the situation changes is an important attribute of a leader. The direction of all activity taken by a leader depends upon the kind of leadership being exercised, the context of the need for direction, the nature of followers, and the type of goal or product envisioned.

- Adapted from <u>John W. Gardner on Leadership</u>, February 1989

Leadership is Togetherness

I went on a search to become a leader.

I searched high and low. I spoke with authority; people listened but, alas, there was one who was wiser than I, and they followed him.

I sought to inspire confidence, but the crowd responded, "Why should we trust you?"

I postured, and I assumed the look of leadership with a countenance that flowed with confidence and pride. But many passed me by and never noticed my air of elegance.

I ran ahead of the others, pointing the way to new heights. I demonstrated that I knew the route to greatness. And then I looked back, and I was alone.

"What should I do?" I queried. "I've tried hard and used all that I know."

And I sat down and pondered long.

And then I listened to the voices around me. And I heard what the group was trying to accomplish. I rolled up my sleeves and joined in the work.

As we worked, I asked, "Are we all together in what we want to do and how to get the job done?"

And we thought together, and we fought together, and we struggled towards our goal.

I found myself encouraging the fainthearted. I sought the ideas of those too shy to speak out.

I taught those who had little skill. I praised those who worked hard.

When our task was completed, one of the group turned to me and said, "This would not have been done but for your leadership."

At first I said, "I didn't lead. I just worked with the rest."

And then I understood: leadership is not a goal ... it is a way of reaching a goal.

I lead best when I help others to go where we've decided we want to go.

I lead best when I help others to use themselves creatively.

I lead best when I forget about myself as a leader and focus on my group, their needs, and their goals.

To lead is to serve ... to give is to achieve together.

- Anonymous

A Work Ethic Philosophy:
Time Segments

To be productive in today's employment arena, you, the essential worker, has to budget time usage and manage personal and professional involvement will colleagues, administrators, and the expectations of all others in day-to-day activities. To do all of what is expected of you in the time established for you at your place of employment oftentimes seems like a plodding, uphill battle based upon your own personal use of time to approach your daily tasks. You may, in fact, have to change the way you work to perform your duties to the best of your ability.

How do employers and employees make the most of the limited time each day to succeed? Here is what workers destined for greatness do which, in fact, might be quite a bit different from what you now do for your company. They prepare and practice all aspects of their work in a distinctive pattern. Many put in long hours per week, as you do, but they don't perform by using hour upon hour of preparation; instead, they break up their work day into a series of shorter, segmented time sessions, or segments, each lasting about eighty or ninety minutes, with perhaps half-hour breaks in between.

Add up these time segments and you will observe approximately four to five hours a day of prime activity. In essence, each day becomes more productive, even though you feel that you are working less. Each day will become an opportunity for you to present a stronger and more efficient effort when it is needed. To use time well is a crucial skill in the workplace, not based upon the time available to you, but by recognizing and using all available resources (mental and physical) for skillful productivity. Preparation is essential, yes, but your ability to sustain the concentration necessary for deliberate and purposeful outcomes means that you will need to "recharge your batteries" throughout the day in order to keep a sharpness and keenness about you.

The concept of using timed segments towards a personal or a corporate goal is not a new idea. For example, you have heard the lament of the high school or college student who complains to his or her teacher or parents, saying "I studied for eight hours straight for this test and still got a C-!" That student believed that "X number of hours of preparation equals a high grade," but educational scientists have determined that any studying continually for a long period of time results in the "law of diminishing returns." After a few hours, a student will not be as receptive to work, both mentally and physically, and, therefore, the latter stages of a lengthy study session will be basically unproductive.

Don't misunderstand the need for rest after each basic preparation time segment. This doesn't mean taking a nap on the job; rather, it is a reference for you to distinguish "work" from "play" and pulling yourself away from a task at regular intervals to something completely different (i.e., "recharging your batteries"). While you set up your break-away periods, keep in mind that you need to get regular rest, eat regularly, and engage in your community normally, and your focus will become that much sharper when you need it to be.

If you have a tendency to fixate on the tasks at hand or assume that your intellectual sharpness will come from caffeine or substances such as stimulants and the like, you will not be as productive in ways expected of you. Many people like to concentrate on the most obvious measurable form of work and try to make those more productive by using stimulants to make them more productive. They should be telling themselves that there are other more established ways to improve performance. There is no question that using time segments effectively rather than rely upon lengthy preparation periods will show stronger results in your work. Like anything else, segmenting preparation periods takes time to learn and incorporate into your daily routine. Once you establish a new preparation regimen, you will wonder how you were ever productive before!

- Adapted from an article that originally appeared in Nautil.us

The Importance of Pedagogy
in the Business World

When you are the lead instructor at your firm and need to train others in your workplace domain, are you aware of, not just the product you are refining, but the process of creating a team and linking it to the aims and goals of your company? Your product cannot sell itself without those under you, and with you, seeing and feeling the process of creation and involvement. This process is known as *pedagogy*, and it cannot be taken for granted in research and development.

Pedagogy, according to the New Oxford American Dictionary, is the method and practice of teaching, especially as an academic subject or theoretical concept. Think back to the exceptional teachers and professors you encountered in high school and college; in many cases it was not always the content of their instruction that made a difference in your learning – it was the way they taught and how they made you eager to learn. An individual needs to capture that process and use it in presentations and programs. A wise professor once said that eighty percent of good teaching is persuasive acting, and that will help learning occur effectively when experts and novices work together for a common product or goal. In this way co-workers are motivated to assist one another. How can this be done? The teacher must also realize that he/she is also the learner when assessing if the "message" sent is being understood and incorporated into the workplace. Working with this thought in mind allows dialog which fosters language, meaning, and values in the context of immediate issues. This joint productive activity is essential in training and development while allowing those instructed to "own" or "buy into" the bigger company picture.

How can a trainer or instructor know when a joint productive activity is working? That individual must create instructional activities requiring trainee collaboration to accomplish a joint product and match the demands of the joint productive activity to the time available for accomplishing them. The arranging of training groups and accommodating a variety of instructional scenarios are essential techniques in having trainees to work in a variety of groupings and move from one activity to another and from larger groupings to smaller ones, as the instruction dictates. Trainees must also have access to materials and technology to facilitate their development while also establishing criteria for monitoring and supporting their growth.

Emphasizing areas of group expression must be given a high priority in team development. The use of language reception and expression must not be overlooked. The two receptive skills of language acuity - Reading and Listening – are often overlooked or assumed to be already well developed within trainees. Yet, the key to learning anything is to listen carefully, associate thoughts about a subject, and develop an answer or opinion. The instructor must learn to use his or her pedagogical skills to sharpen these two skills in trainees. The two expressive skills of language acuity – Speaking and Writing – allow a trainee to produce what he or she knows and to convince others that he or she has something to say. The end result of this is to cultivate the ways language can be used to convince others that what is said is important and relevant, especially in ways of asking and answering questions, challenging claims, and using representations.

The instructor has much to learn in this process, as well. In assisting written and oral language development, the instructor must use "acting" skills such as modeling, eliciting, probing, restating, clarifying, questioning, and praising to ensure that all trainees are getting the appropriate message. Skills such as wait-time eye contact, turn-taking, and respect for others' opinions must not be taken for granted. An emphasis should also be placed upon content vocabulary to further incorporate a trainee into the business "family."

Keeping the trainee focused on the context of the business can be done by consistently emphasizing the trainee's previous knowledge of skills. That is the true meaning of "understanding" a particular role in a particular business. Through this expanded understanding, the trainee will undergo instruction that is cognitively challenging; that is, instruction that requires thinking and analysis at a higher level than rote, repetitive, detail-oriented processes.

Pedagogical instruction, therefore, asks a trainer or instructor to develop an awareness that trainees see the whole picture as a basis for understanding its parts, present challenging standards for performance evaluation, design instructional tasks that advance trainee understanding to more complex levels, assist trainees to accomplish more complex understanding by building from their previous success, and give clear, direct feedback regarding the skills learned in relation to the company's overall mission. The more trainers reduce the distance between themselves and their trainees the greater the understanding of each other's experiences and ideas as they relate to the greater good of the workplace.

- Adapted from "Five Standards of Effective Pedagogy," Center for Research on Education, Diversity, and Excellence, University of California

Authentic Assessment in the Workplace

In order to realistically assess the performance of both employees and employers, consider these initial concerns:

Over 50 % of college students declaring a major course of studies are not practicing in their selected field after their graduation!

There is almost no correlation between grades in school and success in life!

So, how do businesses evaluate and train their workers in areas deeper than the specialty they were hired for? The reality is that the assessment processes used by both business and industry must take into account the underlying factors of innate ability, options for choices, decision making skills, and product accountability for all workers to insure that the workplace will be well run.

The characteristics of a good assessment system for co-workers all concern the influences that motivate the worker and how they can be identified, explored, and utilized. Any system established to increase productivity must be based upon significant and deliberate learning objectives. Also, these characteristics must provide crystal-clear criteria for success, along with good models of what an accomplished goal looks like, and these must be shown at the beginning of instruction. Furthermore, an appropriate system must use tasks that approach or simulate real-life experiences whenever possible. All co-workers must be involved intimately in self-assessment, collaborative critique procedures, and constant re-evaluation of goal-setting. All involved in this plan must be aware of using multiple means of gathering data and establishing and processing a sound record-keeping procedure which can be easily disseminated with other departments and colleagues, thereby operating informative reporting systems. The basis of all assessment sharing that is conducted must meet the criteria of technical soundness.

Here's what should influence a business-planning model: Workers must be prompted to increase performance through these factors:

... on what they are taught/demonstrated to do

... on what it is that they are taught/demonstrated to do

... on how much time is spent on topic presentation and analysis

... on activities co-workers are asked to do on a daily basis

... on how clear co-workers are on what they are doing, why they are doing it, and how focused and motivated they are to do it

An organization-wide action plan must be put into place with these key factors in mind for all workers. First, teaching teams must be established with a company-wide assessment philosophy. Then, an on-going analysis of the effects of these assessment procedures on work-place practices needs to occur periodically. Only in this way can a business establish high standards of performance for all!

If assessments are established for company criteria, then how are these assessments themselves evaluated as to their effectiveness? A strong suggestion is to set up a series of rubrics, or evaluative criteria, based upon each activity used, give a working title for the activity analyzed, specify the qualities on which a piece or type of work will be assessed, define what quality of work earns a given score, and set up a matrix form (perhaps a series of boxes or checklists) for data collection.

Employers need to be aware of successful "best practices" for assessment analyses and re-evaluation, if needed. Always in the fore-front should be their motivation to give clear and deliberate learning objectives for what co-workers should know and be able to do, provide high-quality work and learning experiences to support learning and productivity, and construct clear criteria as assessment tasks to assist colleagues' understanding of how the objectives of a particular learning cycle are met.

What are the factors influencing authentic tasks and what can be used as benchmarks of progress? Be sure that there are clear images of what colleagues are supposed to be able to do and ensure that there are successful models that sample what are expected of colleagues (examples of "the real thing").

All co-workers are to be assessed through the following factors influencing authentic tasks. They will be expected to:

… show interest and motivation

… to construct meaning

… demonstrate important "habits of mind"

… pursue multiple modes of expression

… free themselves from arbitrary constraints

… see progress measured over time

… recognize standards of assessment clearly before a task is undertaken

… receive prompt and useful feedback

So, in summary, all authentic assessment must be composed of the following key points:

Establish criteria for success

Identify and specify levels of performance

Select and display examples of performance levels

Construct personal authentic tasks with clearly understood purposes

Attempt to create reliability among other colleagues/ co-workers

Many companies and corporations recognize the above suggestions as aspects of "Research and Development," and many give only lip-service to the fact that R and D is being carried out. It is sad to say that, because of budget constraints, R and D is usually one of the first areas of a business to be un-funded or underfunded. When they cut back, they lose way more than they could gain. Authentic assessment goes a long way to make businesses grow; re-visit it now!

How to Increase Your Usefulness within Your Company by Following These Ten Guidelines

Do you often wonder what kind of an impact you and your work are having within the company with which you work? Oftentimes, you go about doing your job without receiving any feedback as to how you are doing and how you are perceived by other colleagues or superiors. There are ten guidelines, or checkmarks, that you need to have constantly in mind as you perform your duties. If you are aware of these attitudes that you bring to work each day, your performance will exceed even your highest expectations.

1. <u>Be Patient</u>: Everything that you do will not be always apparent to those who need to know of your results. If you feel confident that what you are doing is worthwhile, stick with your process, and the product may be just what is needed.
2. <u>Be Quiet</u>: This attitude may be difficult at first but "feel out" your situation before venturing an opinion. You actually may want to refine or adjust your approach while listening to and feeling out the tone and mood of a situation.
3. <u>Be Open to Criticism</u>: When you do venture an opinion, be prepared for others who may not agree with your stance. It may

be that their comments could shed light onto your points and assist you in expanding or deepening your point of view.

4. <u>Be Sensible</u>: Keep an open mind about your ideas and discuss any new ideas with logic and acuity. With this attitude you will be listened to and looked upon more favorably by all with whom you interact.

5. <u>Be Flexible</u>: Realize that what you are thinking and saying may need revisions and/or adjustments. Accept change and be willing to re-think ideas that may make your points even more poignant.

6. <u>Be Prepared</u>: Enter into any discussion with as much background material and factual items that may assist you in further topic refinement. Keep the mindset that any points you make may be refuted and may need further clarification.

7. <u>Be Persistent</u>: When you present ideas or information that you fully believe in, be firm and accept dialog as a way to improve your status. Your co-workers will respect your insistence and will assist you in a possible re-working of your ideas for the good of the company.

8. <u>Be Disciplined</u>: As you listen and participate in your work environment, discipline yourself to stay focused on the agenda and/or your duties and keep your level of concentration high. Remember – Attention is not Concentration! Keep your "eye on the prize."

9. <u>Be Confident</u>: If you are the least bit hesitant about your process or product, you will not be able to see your points through to a satisfying conclusion. Know your strengths and your weaknesses and work to overcome any shortcomings you may have. If you do not believe that what you say has merit, why say it at all?

10. <u>Be Enthusiastic</u>: Be sure that your significant points of discussion and interpretation are enthusiastically embraced and are presented in a forthright manner. Bolster your oral statements with accurate grammar and syntax and your written statements with careful proofreading. Even if your presentation is good, poor linguistics may thwart your intentions.

There they are – the ten Be-Attitudes of Business; the guidelines for success in the employment arena.

In addition to the above items, here is what will occur for you if you stay aware of your role in your company. You will become the type of worker your business expects of you in this way:

- As an IDEAL worker, you meet and even exceed standards set by your industry, your company superiors, and your work demands.
- As an ANALYTIC worker, you use observation techniques to record how well they are meeting your personal and performance intentions.
- As an EFFECTIVE worker, you noticeably bring about higher standards for all colleagues.
- As a DUTIFUL worker, you perform your assigned tasks at a high level noticeable by all.
- As a COMPETENT worker, you meet and exceed milestones that indicate you possess requisite performance attributes.
- As an EXPERT worker, you evidence extensive and accessible knowledge and can do more in less time.
- As a REFLECTIVE worker, you learn to examine the process and product of your field to become a more thoughtful practitioner.
- As a SATISFYING worker, you please colleagues, supervisors, and administrators.
- As a DIVERSITY-RESPONSIVE worker, you are sensitive to all co-workers and their environment.
- As a RESPECTED worker, you possess and demonstrate qualities regarded as virtues by all in your environment.

This is your work ethic, your mantra for success. Now is the time for you to perform what is expected of you. You can make a difference in the workplace!

How to Engage More Fully When Attending Corporate Meetings and/or Zoom Conferences

I do not have to tell you that, since the Covid-19 pandemic, the atmosphere of the work arena has undergone a momentous change. Many of us are now working, either partially or fully, from home, and still are expected to keep up with the workplace demands on a daily basis. This change in job approach presents a newer and different challenge for those who need to involve colleagues, clients, and others, and necessitates a re-visiting of certain skills which you probably last used in college classrooms or dorms which now need to be to be applied to today's environment. Below are thirteen hints for taking effective boardroom notes. Some of what follows seem like good common sense, but other points bear repeating and rethinking. It is now time to sharpen your skills involved in listening and speaking as well as in reading and writing.

1. <u>Get Down a Written Transcript of Each Meeting</u> – As you listen to the proceedings of a conference, take down as complete a record of what you hear so you can master the material. How expansive a note-taker are you? It is better to take down too much than too little. Sharpen your listening skills, especially if you are not physically present at the session presentation.

2. <u>Select a Seat or a Room Area Where You Can See and Be Seen</u> – Take a conference room seat or a camera-angle seat where you can be clearly visible from the waist up. Keep up a positive and attentive attitude while listening and writing (typing, if on a laptop). Even if the meeting is tedious, push yourself to keep involved. Think about some of your most strenuous college classes. Remember that the "deadlier" the session is, the more reason you must keep alert and concentrate on the information being provided.

3. <u>Get as Much Information as Possible about the Topic Discussed before the Meeting -</u> Any advanced reading and research you can do in advance will result in your listening and taking notes more easily and with greater understanding. When the subject of the session becomes involved, write more and with more complete thoughts.

4. <u>Have a Method for Recording Your Notes</u> – If you are taking notes in longhand fashion, use a full sheet of paper and do not write on the back of any page. Write legibly! If you are typing, keep significant sections of the presentation under separate tabs for better and more effective editing afterwards. In either format, be sure to note the date and time of the session for future reference and save space between key sections of your transcription for additions and clarifications when you review your work. Leave space at the top of the page and in the left-hand margin for annotation, as well.

5. <u>Take down Your Notes in Outline Form, If Possible</u> – Remember: a new topic = a new page. Indent your transcription to show levels of importance:

    MAIN POINTS ...
        Secondary (Supporting) points ...
          More sub-details ...

Be sure to skip some space when a speaker moves to a new topic. Indentation and "white space" further help with organization and review.

6. <u>Watch for Signals of Importance from the Speaker</u> – Note this: *If something is important enough for a presenter to place on a screen or a board, it is imperative for you to get these points into your notes!* Annotate your transcription by marking **OB** or **OS** (On Board or On Screen) in the margin. Also, during the course of a presentation, learn to know the speaker's vocal inflections. The voice may become slower or louder, so use these verbal clues to get every word said down in your notes and underline a significant vocal shift using your own personal shorthand (underlining, arrows, asterisks, etc.).

7. <u>Listen for the Speaker's Key Phrases</u> – All speakers are intent upon making a point or a series of major ideas. Listen for phrases such as:

    "This is an important reason …"
    "Pay special attention to …"
    "Don't forget that …"

    If the speaker repeats a point, you must assume it is extremely important. Also, listen carefully for examples, illustrations, and definitions. Notate them in your own words, if necessary, for completely clarity.

8. <u>Be Sure to Write down the Details that Connect or Explain Main Points</u> – A good presenter will link areas of a presentation to previous points mentioned or preview points to be taken up further on in the lecture. As you listen, think of the relationship among the major points while you take notes. Record explanations, either word-for-word or in your own words, for clarity. Take advantage of any connection speakers make at the beginning or end of the presentation. Listen carefully for previews or summaries such as:

    "Here's what to look for …"
    "In conclusion/In summary …"

9. <u>Again, Leave Blank Spaces in Your Notes for Any Items or Ideas You Miss</u> - Use the following resources for filling in the "blank" material you might have missed:

    The presenter afterwards, if available …

A colleague who is also present at the same session …

Any backup material (a text, other written information, etc.) …

10. <u>Do Not Hesitate to Ask Questions if the Situation Allows for Them</u> – If certain points are confusing to you, do not be afraid to present yourself and ask for clarification. You could even ask the presenter to phrase a particular point in another way. In fact, many presenters will look favorably upon an inquisitive listener! Most importantly, keep involved in the flow of the proceedings.

11. <u>If There Is a Discussion Period During or After or the Conclusion of the Presentation, Do Not Stop Taking Notes!</u> – Many valuable ideas and clarifications may arise during the more informal give-and-take of a presentation. These ideas make assist you greatly in a more total understanding of the scope and level of a session. This may be a new skill to many of you, but you must *learn to write while you listen!*

12. <u>Be Aware of Any Increasing Tiredness or Notetaking Fatigue as the Presentation Concludes</u> – Note that speakers may feel the need to "speed up" or rush their concluding statements towards the end of a session. Therefore, certain items or points may be presented in a more haphazard manner, perhaps because of time constraints. Be ready to write or type as rapidly as you can to get everything understood and in your notes. You must resist the fatigue that may settle in at this time. Keep your mind on the presentation throughout.

13. <u>Go over Your Notes Soon after the Session</u> – While the session is still clear in your mind, revise your notes as clearly as possible through careful editing and annotating. Tomorrow or next week may be too late for accurate recall. Focus on making sure that your punctuation is clear, your spelling is accurate (especially for technical terms), and unfinished sentences are completed. This is the time to incorporate additional marginal notes and/or annotations to clarify material while the ideas of the session are fresh in your mind.

Above all, realize that good notetaking is a critical and sophisticated skill that constantly needs improvement. A key realization for you to make is that attention is not concentration; you need to work at this skill with total focus. Use all four levels of your personal language acuity: reading and listening (your *receptive* skills) along with speaking and writing (your *expressive* skills). One or more of these four areas may not yet be a strength for you, but all four can be upgraded, once you recognize what you can improve upon.

The Key to Information Recall?
Take Marginal Notes

All of us at one time or another have had to digest a piece of writing for school or business, and many readers don't understand the process of learning material through the effective use of marginal notetaking, or annotating, to enhance memory use and recall techniques. Rather than become baffled by the amount or depth of the material to be understood, focus on these general concepts and employ the annotation procedures I outline below.

Why should you take marginal notes (i.e., writing in the right or left margins or actually onto the text)? First, as you synthesize the document to be read and digested, you must realize that you job as a reader/reviewer is to isolate key segments from what is stated, reduce the writing to basic information, and mentally organize the information so that it becomes more readily understood by you. This general process will assist you in identifying key concepts and more carefully monitor your learning.

What are marginal notes? This technique is an active form of notetaking incorporating the paraphrasing of a writer's main idea(s) and summarizing the key details, while noting, understanding, and learning key terminology essential for accurate recall. Your annotations then should clearly serve as a *study guide* for review and discussion.

What should you write in the margins or within the text? Here's what to focus on: definitions, examples, high or stressed points, people/

dates/places/events, numbered lists of characteristics, main idea with key details, relationships between/among concepts, and any supporting visuals (graphs, charts, diagrams). This is a lot to digest unless you follow a procedure: first, read the written material first without a pen or pencil in your hand in order to get the general idea of the document. Try to reduce the reading to a section-by-section organization of your own while mentally taking note of areas of interest to you. As you complete this first cursory read-through, constantly ask yourself, *Is this information important or significant?* Then in a second reading begin to notate information <u>in your own words</u> as you abridge each section read. *Do not* copy information word for word as you will only need to clarify information later. In a second reading, you need to come away with a general understanding of the information presented. *If you don't understand the information given, you cannot annotate!*

Here's how to implement a thorough marginal notetaking procedure for quick and accurate recall. Then in the second reading begin to notate information <u>in your own words</u> as you abridge each section read. *Do not* copy information word for word as you will only need to clarify information later. Now, with pen or pencil in hand, read the introduction, if offered. It will usually hold valuable clues of the author's intention(s). Then, activate your mind by recalling if you already have any background knowledge of the topic addressed. As you now read more thoroughly, set a purpose for your involvement with the material. Change the title and other headings, if used by the author, to a question which you will attempt to answer through your annotations. Try to notice the author's *organizational patterns* (chronological order, comparison/contrast, cause/effect) and structure your recall around these relationships. Remember to read a short section at a time and be able to isolate the main ideas through your own phrasing. You may have to review and even re-read more difficult sections for clarity.

As you become more adept at marginal notetaking, you may be able to develop your own descriptors and shorthand markings you are comfortable with and will use again. Phrases such as <u>def</u> (definition), <u>ex</u> (example), <u>#</u> (numbered items), <u>*</u> (extremely important), <u>?</u> (needs further explanation), and whatever else you can determine are all good indicators of key information. If you get confused in a section, go back to a heading or topic sentence and ask yourself, *What is the author trying to tell me here?*

As you read while annotating, **selectively underline** main ideas and key supporting details within the text itself, but **do not** underline entire sentences. The key here is to isolate key terms and definitions, transitional words (ex., words that signal an organizational pattern while moving the reader from one thought to another), words/ideas that describe and explain, important lists, and unknown words or terminology (which you can learn through context clues or a dictionary).

Think of this five-step process, called **SQ3R**, to see if you have annotated the material well: **S = Survey** (your first reading to get the main idea), **Q = Question** (turning headings/topic sentences into questions you'll need to answer), **R = Read** (use at least a second reading to annotate the material), **R = Recite** (pose personal answers to your sectional questions), and **R = Review** (re-read/re-think any problematic areas).

How do you know what is important to mark/annotate? Look for stressed words or ideas in the writing and note them. You may ask, *Doesn't annotating take a lot of time?* Yes, it does in the beginning. If you annotate appropriately, you will not have to re-read an author's work in its entirety in preparation for a meeting or discussion. In the end, annotating will actually save you time and energy while enhancing comprehension.

Here are some cautions to take while annotating. Be careful of ... The "Medieval Monk" Syndrome (copying everything word for word), The "Nothin' Here" Syndrome (not much is extracted from the text, or just random details and ideas jotted here and there), or The "Rest of the Story" Syndrome (annotating key topics but no connected ideas or thoughts).

Like anything else worth doing, this procedure takes practice; in fact, you may recall doing this type of procedure in high school or college. This thinking process is indispensable in today's business world, and all companies which depend on strong inter- and intra-office communications should actually instruct all workers to deal with all written material in this way.

Using this process will enhance productivity!

- Adapted from Reading/Humanities, Brookdale College, Lincroft, New Jersey

How to "Read" People in the Workplace Using Inferential Reasoning Techniques

In order to avail yourself of crucial decision-making tools as you make daily adjustments to your work day, it becomes essential to analyze your personnel and others with whom you have business. A key ingredient in determining a course of action is to understand as much about co-workers and business associates as you can when interacting with them. Using inferential reasoning will go a long way towards getting a sense of whom you are dealing with and how you and they are also dealing with an idea. Your knowledge of inferences and their place in your personal skill subset must continue to be developed to help you as you assess the meaning of others.

You can draw many conclusions from those around you by concentrating on another's presentation of information for your analysis. Look carefully at how a person presents himself/herself to you when you first meet. Look at personal activity ("body language") which will tell you a lot about another's mindset at the time of interaction. Get to know as much about one's lives outside of the office as you can as subtly as you can. You can often infer quite a bit about others from their day-to-day work habits. What do they own, collect, or want? You must be sensitive to what others "bring to the table" and draw conclusions from any hints or points that you can determine as that, essentially, is inferential reasoning. Great leaders and heads of business and industry have honed this interpretative skill to a point where their decision-making capabilities are sharp and accurate. Their sensitivity to how others appear to them through the five senses creates a vivid picture, as well, of how each may act, especially in certain situations.

Here are some ways to sharpen your inferential reasoning. Think about what you know of this individual from what others may have said to you or what a resume or presentation may say about him/her. Learn to "read between the lines" and draw inferences based upon the facts you have at your disposal and extend your thinking beyond that realm.

Also, think about how a person conveys himself/herself to you either in person or in writing. People often reveal a great deal about themselves and about what is going on in their lives by what they say, the way they say something, and perhaps by what they don't say.

More often than not, business leaders are asking new hiring candidates and even established workers to complete a writing sample about a given scenario to see how they would react to the prompt.

In addition, pay close attention to how an individual with whom you are interacting opens a conversation or answers a question to get an idea of that person's sense of organization and presentation ability. See if points made are supported through expansion and sound conclusions.

Remember, your goal in any type of personal interaction is to learn more about another than you did previously, especially in order to give that person more viable guidelines under which to work or continue work. So often in a given day, a leader needs to draw sound conclusions from hints or facts while thinking about others. Inferential thinking is actually inferential reasoning. We all do it to some extent, but can we do it better?

LANGUAGE

To Communicate is to Educate!

According to Diane Ravich, Educational Historian, the single biggest problem in American education is that *no one agrees on why we educate* the way we do. So, why must we educate? We educate because we want citizens who are capable of taking responsibility for their lives and for our democracy. We must have citizens who understand how their government works and who are knowledgeable about the history of our nation and other nations. We need citizens who are thoroughly educated in the sciences, and we need people who can communicate in our language as well as in other languages. We must ensure that every young person has the chance to engage in the arts.

But, because of our narrow-minded utilitarianism, Ravich continues, we have forgotten what good education is.*

To paraphrase author Noah Hawley, we have forgotten how important hope is in our lives. He says that we need hope to form a thought and to engage in meaningful conversation. Because, as Hawley states, otherwise, what is the point of any communicating at all? What difference does it really make what we say to each other?**

We all have feelings which we need to get out in the open. That's the real essence of communication. Charles Frazier, another noted novelist, speaks of this notion through one of his characters: "And for so long I have hated my nature for failing to say what I felt. And most of all for not acting on it. You live with such choices until you die. They eat at you like heartworm, coring you out until you are just skin enclosing nothing. A balloon filled with hot breath."***

So we must continue to get our thoughts out and down – out in our speech and down on paper. If we keep our present levels and methods of communication, we have short-changed our own education as well as that of others. This is what education is – a dialog with humanity, maybe eliciting disagreement, yet, as Winston Churchill once famously stated, "Dialog is more important than consensus."****

When you speak, you educate; when you listen, you are educated. The great educator, John Dewey, once concluded that "…Education is not preparation for life; education is life itself."*****

In the words of the noted psychologist, B. F. Skinner, "Education is what survives when what has been learned has been forgotten."******

We have a great social responsibility to deal with education in order to prepare to communicate and educate; this is human growth. Allow this responsibility into your lives; give your inner thoughts and feelings a chance to be explored by others. Fully embracing education in all its forms will allow you to use the four great gifts of language inherent to you: to read, to listen, to speak, and to write. There can be no greater statement of this conviction than these words spoken by Thomas Jefferson:*******

"Educate and inform all of the people, for they are the source of our strength and our freedom."

Diane Ravich, "The New York Times Magazine," September 27, 2009
**Noah Hawley, <u>Before the Fall</u>*
***Charles Frazier, <u>Thirteen Moons</u>*
****Winston Churchill: "Dialogs"*
*****John Dewey (quoted in Bookreporter.com)*
******B. F. Skinner (quoted in Heavy.com)*
*******Thomas Jefferson: "Papers"*

Language Acuity/Levels of Language

In order to improve yourself and be taken seriously by others around you, you must recognize and develop what I call your *Language Acuity*. Each of us has four types of language acuity which can be categorized as Reading, Listening, Writing, and Speaking.

The first two – Reading and Listening - are your **Receptive Skills**, as they are the skills that you develop from other communicators who want to tell you something. You are taking in their information in order to analyze and synthesize it at a particular time and place and for a particular reason or purpose. As you read and as you listen, you interpret message and meaning to determine what may be useful to you.

The third and fourth type – Writing and Speaking – are your **Expressive Skills**, as they are the skills that you develop from the first two skills in order to tell something of what you know to others. These must be honed carefully as they tell others that you have something to say that contains meaning and expects reaction and response from those with whom you interact.

I tell college students often that their receptive skills have gone a long way towards getting them into their next level of learning, but their expressive skills now must work towards getting them out of their present level and into the next. Students must feel confident in that they have something to say and something to contribute. I say to my first-year students that their receptive skills, for the most part, got them into college, but their expressive language skills will get them out! They must prove that what they have to say is poignant enough to others so that they will listen and react accordingly. I say further to them that college has three major milestones: first, college is a hell of a hard place to get into; second, college is a hell of a hard place to stay in; and third, college is a hell of a hard place to get out of with a degree. They have succeeded in overcoming the first obstacle; the second and third will draw on their ability to convince others that they have something to say! Much of the above scenario applies equally as well to the workplace.

Each of us also has *Levels of Language* which aids in our communication at a given time and place and to a given audience. There are three levels of sophistication that relate to our receptive and expressive language usage. Our basic and most easily referenced language is the **Vulgate** level of usage. We don't need to be taught this; this is "street language," or "text talk," or social media "emoticons." It could mean coarse or gross, as the actual term implies, but it is basically the primary form of communication that individuals use in a casual manner.

All of us in any walk of life need to aspire to the next level of language which is **Media**. This is the level of modern, acceptable communication which is to be used when we are interacting with acceptable levels of media, such as corresponding with others in a cordial professional manner. Letters, job reports, evaluations, and the like must be presented at this level for proper acceptance.

The highest level of language, to which most of us aspire but few of us attain, is the level of **Poetry**. This is life-lifting language used to lift up our spirits and inspire more abstract thoughts and concepts than could be shown through the media level. This process is also the ability to "play with language" and manipulate it towards a higher order of meaning. The creation of imagery and symbolism is paramount in poetic communication.

Each of these levels should act as a check-point in language growth and development. When I work with my college-age students, I constantly have to remind them to rise above the vulgate wording of a piece of writing and move solidly towards the media level of communication whenever a seriousness of purpose is warranted.

Why the Art of Punctuating
Properly is So Important

The art of proper punctuation is often one of the most overlooked of all the writing skills that one can attain and use. The use of a comma, a semi-colon, a colon, and the like should not be an author's haphazard choice, and, if improperly used, can result in possible misinterpretation and confusion by a reader looking for appropriate information.

Probably the least understood of all punctuation marks is the comma. In an article entitled "New Sentences," by Sam Anderson (*The New York Times Magazine, March 26, 2017)*, this distinguished writer gives good advice, as he states:

> Never underestimate a comma. A comma can do anything. It can divvy up your most complex thoughts as precisely as a butcher cleaves a cow into prime and subprime cuts of beef. It can be a paper bag that allows your hyperventilating mind to breathe. Commas are the nails, rivets, screws, joints, braces, brackets, hinges, pins, and pegs in the vast architecture of human thought. Lose one, and the whole structure will threaten to rattle apart. Hazards abound. A sentence with a missing comma is a horse trailer coming unhitched on a highway at 70 miles an hour. A sentence with an extra comma is a boulder in your swimming pool.

Let's look at a practical example of why punctuation matters in the following scenario:

> In Ohio a woman beat a traffic ticket by calling out her town's bad grammar. Andrea Cammelleri found her truck towed from a spot where "… motor vehicle campers, …" were prohibited, but the citation should have read "… motor vehicles, campers, …". Cammelleri told a judge that her truck was not a "motor vehicle camper, and that the ticket was incorrect. The judge agreed and ordered the town to pay her $1,500. "I was told 'Don't fight City Hall, as I'd never win. But I did," she said. (*The Week Magazine, September 11,2015*)

Where you place a comma or commas in a sentence is not arbitrary. There are certain "rules" that come into play, many more than can be listed here. However, the *Modern Language Association (MLA)* does set certain guidelines for appropriateness. For example, read this:

At the store, I bought eggs, bacon, bread, and butter. (MLA format)

> At the store, I bought eggs, bacon, bread and butter. (New York Times format)

The New York Times is not considered "scholarly writing," so their format is frowned upon by most editors and copywriters. The simple rule is this: always have one less comma than the number of items you are listing (four items bought = three commas). MLA does not want to encourage a reading of the sentence where "bread and butter" could be misconstrued as a single bought object.

Also, read these sentences:

> Because I was sick, I stayed home.
> I stayed home because I was sick.

Both sentences are punctuated correctly! Each sentence says the same thing but in reverse order which makes a difference in the comma usage. The first sentence uses "Because I was sick" as an introductory clause, but it is not a complete thought, and therefore it is considered subordinate in nature and not the main clause of the sentence. In the second sentence, the writer begins with the complete thought (main clause) and concludes with the secondary, or subordinate, clause. Therefore, the subordinate clause is no longer introductory, and setting it off from the rest of the sentence by a comma is not needed

Don't be a "comma casualty!" Know what you want to say and how to say it correctly. If you become "comma-shy," you will probably be in as bad a situation as if you had over-used this skill. Take the advice of Lynne Truss, the highly successful author of *Eats, Shoots and Leaves* (play with a comma or two with that title for two different meanings) who tells us:

> Without punctuation there is no reliable way of communicating meaning. Punctuation herds words together, keeps others apart. Punctuation directs you how to read in the way musical notation directs a musician how to play.

Remember that punctuation can be used in three different ways, and two of them are wrong. It can be used, misused, or abused, and careful attention is needed to correct usage. When committing anything to writing for your company, your boss, and even yourself, review with care how words and phrases can be fused together for the true accuracy that you want.

The Importance of Proper Word Order in Language

"The difference between the almost right word and the right word is really a large matter – 'tis the difference between the lightning bug and the lightning." (*Mark Twain*)

Where you place words in sentences can make a major difference in <u>what</u> you are trying to say and <u>how</u> you are trying to say it.

Let's look at this simple sentence: *I stole my brother's hat.* The meaning is perfectly clear. Now, let's add the word **only.** Look what happens to the meaning of that sentence <u>depending on where you insert the word **only:**</u>

> ***Only*** *I stole my brother's hat.*

What does this sentence actually say? No one else stole the hat; only I did.

> *I* ***only*** *stole my brother's hat.*

What does this sentence actually say? I only stole the hat; I didn't rip it or lose it or do anything to it.

> *I stole* ***only*** *my brother's hat.*

What does this sentence actually say? I stole only the hat; I didn't steal his coat or his gloves or anything else.

*I stole my **only** brother's hat.*

What does this sentence actually say? I have but one brother.

*I stole my brother's **only** hat.*

What does this sentence actually say? My brother has but one hat.

*I stole my brother's hat **only**.*

This sentence cannot ever be said because of the improper word order as it does not make sense and has no meaning.

***

Can you see the word order problem in this sentence, again using the word **only**?

Ray Rice (who played pro football) *was **only** suspended for two games.*

What does this sentence actually say? He was suspended; he wasn't fined or jailed or anything else.

But when the word **only** gets moved to a difference place in the sentence, see how the meaning changes.

*Ray Rice was suspended **only** for two games.*

Now what does this sentence actually say? Two games was the duration of the suspension – no more, no less.

***

Your word choices can also lead to a misunderstanding of your actual intent. Look at this sentence:

He resigned.

What does this sentence actually say? We don't really know! Did he quit his job, or did he sign another, or additional, contract?

Say what you mean, and mean what you say!

Improve Your Company's Writing Profile with Artificial Intelligence (AI)

Do you know that the writing your company generates can be greatly assisted by Artificial Intelligence (AI)? Many schools and colleges use an on-line technique entitled *Grammarly* which acts in similar fashion to another on-line technique entitled *Spellcheck*. *Grammarly*, a tech firm, uses machine learning and artificial intelligence to improve a writer's composition presentation, advancing from basic spelling checks to grammatical accuracy suggestions and syntax recommendations regarding readability and clarity. The app, which can be downloaded to any computer or mobile device, is free of charge while an advanced version adds stylistic changes and other structural recommendations for a fee.

Founded in 2009, the San Francisco-based startup has performed well, so much so that it recently raised $110 million to hire more developers. The *Grammarly* app is available for the Chrome browser, Microsoft Word, and Windows laptop and desktop setups.

In the future, developers hope to improve on its language suggestions to keep pace with the changeability of modern language while still offering suggestions that will present writers with style suggestions from business letters to academic essays. Although *Grammarly* relies on AI, "… it's not for replacing humans," said co-founder Max Lytvyn. "It makes humans more powerful."

> *- adapted from Tomio Geron, the Wall Street Journal*
> *and reported in The Week magazine, May 2017*

No Wonder English is Such a Hard Language to Learn and Use Correctly

As you sit at your computer and try to compose and present your thoughts on a given subject, the function and usage of language doesn't occupy much of your time. Yet, there are many words in English which contain either different pronunciations or different meanings depending on the context you wish to present. I've compiled a list of many of the most common of these words drawn from anonymous sources over the years. Here are just a few:

- The bandage was wound around the wound.
- The farm was used to produce produce.
- The dump was so full that it had to refuse refuse.
- We must polish the Polish furniture.
- He could lead if he could get the lead out.
- The soldier decided to desert his dessert in the desert.
- Since there is no time like the present, he thought it was time to present the present.
- A bass was painted on the face of the bass drum.
- When shot at, the dove dove into the bushes.
- I did not object to the object.
- When did she record the record?

Additionally, let's visit the wacky world of oxymorons. Everyone has said them, and even as you say or hear them, you think … that doesn't make a lick of sense … which doesn't make sense either. Oxymorons are words strung together that make a completely different meaning than does each of the words individually. Try these "more-ons:"

Real Magic	All Alone
Pure Evil	Living Dead
Jumbo Shrimp	Small Crowd
Random Order	Soft Rock
Criminal Justice	New Classic
Same Difference	Found Missing
Government Organization (?)	Passive Aggression
Sanitary Landfill	Plastic Glasses
Civil War	Terribly Pleased
Speed Bump	Genuine Imitation
Definite Maybe	Pretty Ugly
Act Naturally	Diet Ice Cream
Working Vacation	

I'm sure you can think of many others to add to this list.

Let me close with a little English lesson for you. Think of function and usage as you read these statements …

- The words "listen" and "silent" are anagrams (using the same letters).
- The word "race car" is a palindrome (same spelling backwards and forwards).

- The word "eat" is the only word that, if you take the first letter and move it to the last, it spells its past tense ("ate").
- The word "bookkeeper is the only word in the English language that contains three double letters back to back to back.

Have fun with these, but watch out for your language acuity!

WRITING

WRITING

CAMPAIGN

RELATIONSHIPS   COMMUNICATIONS   DIRECTOR

TYPES   PUBLIC RELATIONS   MANAGE
MEDIA

CORPORATE   MEDIA   SPEECHES   GOODWILL
VIRAL

The Art of Argumentation

Arguing a point of view is not easy; you must realize at the outset that most arguments can never seem to be settled (think of *religion* and *politics*). Stanley Fish*, who has studied argumentation for many years, states that argumentation is a necessity of human nature because, as he states, perfect consensus is "… not something we mortals will ever achieve," and that argument is welcome because "… the skills of disputation are the skills by means of which political orders and, indeed, civilizations are built." According to Fish, as Aristotle argued, "… a speaker has three means of persuasion: an appeal to logic *(logos)*, an appeal to the audience's fears and biases *(pathos)*, and the projection of an admirable persona *(ethos)*.

Argumentation is a reasoning process intended to inform and then persuade another. It is based upon logic which appeals to the mind and the intellect. Arguments rely on emotion, careful planning, and a specific thesis, or proposition, to be put forward. Organization of evidence for your point of view should be based upon language choice, rhetorical style, and a substantial conclusion.

There are many argument procedures, all of which should focus on you, the speaker, your subject, and your audience. These are Informal or Explanatory (to tell why a controversy exists), Focused (to change one's mind about something), Action-Oriented (to be highly persuasive), Quiet or Subtle (to show a shaped or slanted piece of evidence), or Reconciliation (to show the "hardening" of a position). The internal structure of your argument could take one of two approaches: an

Inductive Process (developing from a specific or personal point to a general logical conclusion), or a Deductive Process (moving from an overall generality to a more specific or personal conclusion. Oftentimes, *syllogistic reasoning* is used for emphasis, with points or ideas based upon a major (believable) premise, leading to a minor premise, concluding with a given point.

Argumentation is a process of logic and determination which is based upon an assertion, stemming from strong evidence, resulting in a convincing conclusion. Be sure to consider the following process flash-points as you lay out your game plan: strength of introduction/premise/thesis; accuracy of proposition based upon key truths; intended audience of listeners, readers, reactors; supporting evidence which is logical and realistic; use of organizational patterns such as cause-effect and comparison-contrast; and a forceful emphatic conclusion proving your point without a doubt.

Here's how to set up the framework for your argument procedure. In the introduction, state the problem/issue and any background information available. Lead with an objective explanation of the issue/controversy. Specify the *who, what, when, where,* and *why* as well as the *how.* Present facts, quotations, and other documentation from sources which are relevant. In the body, provide two to four reasons why you are right and use supporting evidence here. Next, mention any opposing points of view. Identify who opposes you and why you disagree with these viewpoints. Present the opposing information fairly in some depth but then refute them with strong emphasis. Finally, in the solution/conclusion, re-emphasize the main issue and strongly say why your way of thinking is much better. Get strong here … build momentum while you give solutions to the problem or challenge your reader/listener to be better informed. Sometimes it is important to an argument to say "If you don't do …x, y or z, …" to enforce your crucial points.

Remember not to rant and rail at the opposition, as arguing is not a "shouting match." The key to any good sound argument is NOT to be "wishy-washy." Take a stand, take it early, and reinforce it often with FORCE. As a writer, don't forget the use of exclamation points!

Whenever you write or speak to convince, you must defend your point of view as if you were arguing a legal case in front of a judge and jury. Lawyers are taught to defend their client's point of view with information which must convince others that their information is accurate and true "... beyond a reasonable doubt!"

taken from The Week magazine, August 12, 2016
- adapted from Brookdale Community College's
English 121 Instructor's Materials, 2014

Decisions and Choices

How many decisions do you make in a single day? Countless, right? Do you know if you have a method for making decisions? When you opt for performing an action or think about why you decided to do what you do, you are using a little-know skill known as *metacognition*. Very few of us actually do this as this term means "to think about thinking." Could this make a difference in your decision-making? Should it? Most of us don't spend enough time actually determining how the mind works in decision-making situations. Ask these questions of yourself:

Can you always think before you act?

Can you predict how you will act?

Can you predict why you would act?

Can you predict the consequences of your action/s?

Know thyself! Remember that all decisions lead to choices, or options, for action. Here are the "A-B-C-D's" of decision-making:

A = ABILITY: God-given basis for all action … leading to …

B = BRAIN: To spark your abilities to think and process … leading to …

C = CHOICES: Brain selection of options available … leading to …

D = DECISION: A course of action based on choices you have.

The timing of your actions is, of course, extremely important. Think of these three scenarios:

If an act is <u>pre-meditated</u>, you are able to select a course of action from options (Should I wear this jacket or that jacket?).

If an act is <u>automatic</u>, you probably have little or no time to think of options (Hitting the brakes in your car).

If an act is <u>spontaneous/split-second</u>, your reaction occurs without thinking (Clapping your hands, Yawning).

But what about the re-action(s) to an action you take? Sometimes you don't take into consideration the results of an action you take. Remember that all actions lead to reactions, and that this process, called *cause and effect,* could be predictable or not. Think about how these terms are used in articles, manuals, or books that you read or write. In a history reading, authors actually use these terms to get you to think about action and reaction:

What were the three <u>causes</u> of the Civil War? What was the <u>effect</u> of Reconstruction on the South?

In a Science reading, think of how much of what you need to process to learn material is based upon a similar principal called stimulus and response:

What would happen if you add Chemical A to Chemical B? You could get Chemical C, you could get nothing (still noted as a response), or you could blow up the lab (not advisable!).

In conclusion, here are three quotes which should be taken very seriously (the first two are attributed to Albus Dumbledore, Headmaster, Hogwarts School for Wizardry – remember the Harry Potter novels and movies):

It is not our abilities which make us who we are; it is our choices.

We must all make a choice between what is right and what is easy

This last quote nicely sums up the "human condition" regarding how we reason as we make choices:

Uncertainty is a key aspect of human reasoning. Without uncertainty we would never doubt ourselves or our decisions. We would be certain that we're right all the time. It's this certainty that can make AI's (Artificial Intelligence) ability to learn turn brittle over time. But if an AI is uncertain and capable of doubt (like a human), it can begin to judge itself, to question whether an action or decision will have the consequence it desires and tests it more thoroughly. In this way, it begins to understand probability – specifically the convoluted relationship between cause and effect.

- Crucible, James Rollins (Chapter 16)

Decision Schema: A Prelude to Adding Strength and Direction to Writing

William Faulkner, a legend among American writers, tells us how to be better writers as follows:

> Anyone who wants to be a writer should be a reader first. Read, read, read everything - trash, classics, good and bad, and see how they do it. Just like a carpenter who works as an apprentice and studies the master, read!

One method which can be used successfully in transitioning from reading analysis to writing ability is to learn how, when, where, and why literary characters make decisions through the course of a plot (see my earlier article about decisions and choices). As you develop as a reader, you will gain an awareness of patterning, or analytical construction and classification seen within many types of literature. As you read anything, look for a series of relationships among, plot, character, setting, and theme with classifiable, therefore more readily understandable, interaction possibilities. Plot complexity, character revelation, implicit/explicit thematic construction, and consistent/ inconsistent point of view will enable the reader to understand further the complex dynamic waiting to be revealed in any piece of literature. Stories "work" because of anticipation, build-up, and prediction which successful authors blend into their works to enhance enjoyment. Try to mirror this kind of movement and direction in your writing as you compose reports, analytical pieces, requests, arguments, and the like.

In order to assist your reader with coming to grips with your written purpose and intention, set up your writing with indicators so that your reader can closely predict the outcome, or outcomes, of your writing. Predicting outcomes is a strategy employed by efficient readers as it involves a willingness by the reader to take risks and creates a necessity for self-monitoring to confirm or reject what he or she has anticipated from the text.

To move towards a predicted outcome, as a reader you must initially develop a clear vision or focus of a character or characters in a story, as you would do in presenting a point of discussion in your own writing. You must always keep the decision or result of your written idea(s) easily interpretable by noting a character's ability to make decisions which, oftentimes, are based on appearance, personality, background, motivation, relationships, conflict, and change. Good readers are able to predict how characters "move along a story line," and that should be the focus of strong and accurate literary analysis and interpretation in order to give the reader the deepest understanding possible from the written document. The following figure is a diagram of the movement of a short story based upon decision schema:

A DIAGRAM OF THE MOVEMENT OF A SHORT STORY
(Decision Schema)

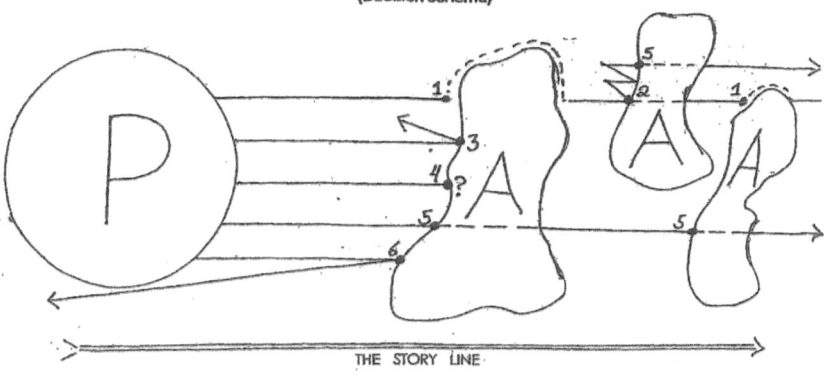

THE STORY LINE

Analysis

P = ProtagonistThe *Prime Mover* in the story

A = Antagonist(s) The *Force* (person, place, thing, or idea) set against the Protagonist

* = Decision(s) The *Pivotal Points* of story movement

1° Protagonist skirts an issue, when confronted, by quick thinking, or alternatives, or diverse action

2° Protagonist confronts Force, backs off, attempts again, and through perseverance, endures

3° Protagonist meets Force and is repelled by it, never to attempt movement again

4° Protagonist confronts Force and hesitates... and hesitates... and is indecisive as to further action (Hamlet figure)

5° Protagonist confronts and defeats an obstacle (many obstacles) and "... lives happily every after" (Noble Savage, Superman, James Bond)

6° Protagonist confronts Force and is so repelled by it that he/she regresses in time and space either mentally or physically or both

This figure represents a schematic of a typical short story (focusing on only a single character) indicating the way a key character, or protagonist develops, or progresses, along a story line from some point of beginning to some point of ending involvement. The protagonist, or prime mover, in a short story, in most instances, cannot progress through this journey without encountering obstacles, or antagonistic situations, designed by the author to impede progress while at the same time allowing the reader to taker a deeper glimpse into the "stuff" of which the protagonist is made. Antagonists, therefore, are forces set against the protagonist, not just to impede progress, but also to allow the reader further insight into how the character is visualized or imagined. The reader needs to notice how a character is revealed by the author. Dramatization, character contrasts, character consistency, motivation, plausibility, and fullness of development are all significant indicators for a reader to experience a total realization and understanding of character development and movement. This type of "text orientation" has resulted in readers understanding more fully the movement of a story or scenario and will prove invaluable to those writing about problems and solutions. An awareness of how characters, such as the protagonist, encounter these antagonists, or antagonistic situations, creates the "moment of decision," which can "make" or "break" an individual (noted by the black *decision point* by each antagonist encountered). I have isolated six possible decision schemes which should be analyzed as pivotal points for an understanding of the significant points of story movement for a reader and a writer to see and experience more completely character and plot interaction and development.

Decision Scheme #1 – The protagonist, when confronted by a force, is able to anticipate the problem and has the ability to avoid, or skirt, the issue by quick thinking, or alternatives, or diverse action. An example could be seen in *Flight*, s classic short story by John Steinbeck. Briefly, a Mexican/Southern Californian youth is sent into town by his mother to purchase supplies (there is no father in the home). In town he is taunted and teased to a point where he loses control and, in a scuffle, kills a person. As he returns home, no longer an innocent child, he knows he will become a wanted man and therefore indicates to his mother and siblings that he must go off into the mountains to avoid the forces set against him. By anticipating the problems he will face, the boy is able to at least postpone them temporarily.

Decision Scheme #2 – The protagonist confronts a force, backs off, attempts again, and through perseverance endures. This character exhibits creative cognitive skills and, in essence, comes up with a "Plan B" which helps overcome the situation. An obvious example would be The Little Engine in the classic story *"The Little Engine That Could."* This struggle using the dedication and perseverance needed to overcome an obstacle is a timeless lesson about "… if at first you don't succeed, try, try again."

Decision Scheme #3 - The protagonist meets a force, takes a course of action, but is repelled by the force, never to attempt movement again. This character, although meeting an unconquerable obstacle and not being able to continue through the story, still maintains influence over others who recall and react to the influence of the non-present protagonist. An example would be Julius Caesar, in Shakespeare's tragedy of the same name, who is assassinated early on in the play but whose "ghost" and specter of power remain throughout the five acts of the play.

Decision Scheme #4 – The protagonist confronts a force and hesitates … and hesitates … and is indecisive as to further action. This character creates an image through failure to act which could lead to stagnation along the story line. An example would be Hamlet, in another of Shakespeare's tragedies, who returns from school in England upon hearing of his father's murder. Although he knows he needs to exact revenge for his father's death, he cannot come up with a plan to murder his uncle, Claudius, the revealed murderer. One notable scene depicts Hamlet raging through the deep cellars of the castle when he happens to see Claudius, alone, praying in one of the underground chapels. Hamlet immediately draws his dagger and walks up behind Claudius, but as he raises his hand to strike, he begins to think and questions to himself: What is Claudius doing now? He is praying. If I kill him now, he will go straight to heaven. That is too good for him! Hamlet sheathes his dagger and leaves the chapel unnoticed.

Decision Scheme #5 – The protagonist confronts and defeats an obstacle (or many obstacles) and "… lives happily ever after." This character embodies the "superman" or "superhero" of literature. An example in early American Literature would be the Noble Savage so well depicted in James Fenimore Cooper's many novels about Indian awareness and dignity through characters such as Chingatchgook and Natty Bumpo. In more recent literature, Ian Fleming's series of James Bond adventures depicts a character who can do no wrong. Bond knows how to fly jets, ski off cliffs, expertly use exotic firearms, and order the correct wine in any country in the world. Realistic? No. Engaging character? Yes.

Decision Scheme #6 – The protagonist confronts a force which is so devastating that he/she regresses in time and space – either mentally, physically, or both – and ends in a far worse situation than at the start. A scenario of this type would be this: a successful middle-aged man returns home one day from work only to find out that his wife has left him and has also taken the children. The next few days as he ruminates around the house trying to determine the reason for his lost home life, he falls into a state of depression. Finally, he reaches the point where he tries to continue at work, but his performance drops, and he is subsequently fired. With no real home to go to, he begins to spend more and more time at a local bar and befriends a sordid group of barflies. As he sinks deeper into despair, one morning the police find him dead, perhaps from suicide.

Each of these situations requires an understanding of the decisions that people make when confronted by problems or concerns. Understanding how people interpret crises and cope with them through decision-making allows an evaluator of writing a wonderful and strong insight into a person's character, motive, and actions.

If you use a piece of writing as an evaluative tool for assessing the abilities of a prospective job candidate or a review of an employee's job performance, you will be able to learn much about how a person approaches life and handles work and, therefore, you can make clearer and more useful determinations as to how a company can best use an individual.

- Donald C. Yates, Associate Professor, Caldwell College (NJ)
- Adapted from an article of his appearing in The New Jersey
Association of Teacher Educators (NJATE) Journal, Fall 2001

Building Strong Narration as an Important Communication Tool

Author's Note: After having taught a course entitled <u>English Composition:</u> <u>The Writing Process</u> at the college level for many years, I would like to share with you some of my insights for your possible usage using the written word as a crucial Expressive Skill to present yourself in the best possible light to another individual or individuals who might want to know something about you through your writing skills. More and more employers are now asking prospective employees to complete a writing sample as a piece of their application process; my suggestions here are what I tell my students to assist them, not only in my class, but also in the world of work.

What is a narrative? Most importantly, it tells a story. It is a recreation of a single experience over time and focuses on a personal experience (past or present) or someone else's experience that you closely shared. The story results in the communication of a main idea or lesson learned from the experience. It makes a point. So, how do you start?

First, you must identify an experience and think of why it is significant. If it is significant to you, then you must make it significant to others. Then, draft carefully your knowledge of the general and specific details and outline the process (the stages of development) before drafting the experience in full detail with powerful and compelling language. I suggest that you use a "cluster" format as an outline in which you center on a piece of paper your Main Topic and then surround that center with ideas arrayed around the central topic as you brainstorm your story's development. You should base each "ray" of your array on People (involvement), Place (situation), Time (significance), and Incident (action and reaction). Your story must conclude with a Learning Experience (a lesson or moral) that others could draw from.

As you mentally prepare your narrative, think of the following key benchmarks for your presentation: wording, sequencing, imagery, and vivid sensual description. Don't just tell the story – use well-worded details and descriptive language to bring the story to life. Create your story by thinking as if something reading the story has **no** background information. Remember that seemingly unimportant details known to you must **come alive** to your readers.

One of the most difficult aspects of all communication is "getting it out" and "getting it down." There are two ways of doing this: (1) you could begin recreating your experience by stating your thesis and setting the framework and importance of the experience, or (2) you could begin immediately with the experience and conclude with its significance. As you start a first draft, be sure to order your information logically and sequence scenes properly for clarity. In fact, you may feel the need to present character dialog to create and enhance a scene or setting.

As you create your story, you need to visualize your experience as you write. Think of writing your experience as if you are writing a movie script, or a screen play, or a scene which will need to be carried over to a movie set and made into film. Imagine yourself as a "movie director" who must visualize the words in print and make them come alive on stage. As a movie director, you have the power to edit or even drop scenes that don't work within the general flow of the story. Finally, even when you think you are done, re-think and re-imagine what you have said for the clarity that you need to put the story across to another.

Here is what to avoid. Don't use abstract language and/or fuzzy terminology. Don't assume your readers have any knowledge of the experience. Don't use long introductory material and lengthy description which has no direction or purpose and may distract a reader's concentration.

Don't simply tell what something is or looks like; use figurative language (similes, metaphors, analogies, personification, alliteration, etc.)

It is a very difficult task to quantify a piece of writing which, in and of itself, is unquantifiable. When I was an English Department chairman of a large urban high school, my teachers would nitpick their critiques of student writing by giving grades of A+, A, A-, B+, B, B-, C+, C, C-, D+, D, D-, and F with nothing more to base grades on but their personal feelings. Some even gave students C++ or D--! At a department meeting I challenged any English teacher in the room to give me a clear distinction between an A- and a B+ paper. They could not do so, and we then agreed to grade papers *holistically*, that is by constructing a *rubric*, or grid, to give a numerical point value to a paper based upon certain agreed-upon criteria. We developed five key criteria upon which to judge all papers and agreed to give a grade for each criterion with one of four numerical values, from 2 (barely proficient) to 5 (highly proficient). An even number of numerical choice values was used so an evaluator could not conveniently seek a "middle ground" in grading.

The five selected criteria were as follows: **Purpose/Introduction/Conclusion** (thesis and framework for the writing), **Organization** (structure and transitional elements), **Supporting Details** (content), **Sentence Structure/Mechanics** (well-chosen wording with proper punctuation, spelling, and capitalization), and **Engagement** (evidence of corrected draft/s and revision/s). Each criterion, after having been assigned a score between 2 and 5, was then multiplied by 4 to result in a numerical total based upon a 100-point scale. Teachers were then asked to present hand-written commentary about the overall impact of the piece of writing.

After a set of papers had been appropriately evaluated, teachers were then asked to compile a list of writing concerns, based upon patterns of writing errors, or improvable areas, noted for each class of students' completed assignments.

Below are some of the concerns teachers noted when an analysis of an initial set of essays regarding the narrative process:

Avoid abbreviations   Avoid slang terms   Don't overexaggerate
Avoid sentence fragments   Avoid run-on sentences   No awkward phrasing

Use "…people who…," not "…people that…"

Don't confuse *than* with *then*, *their* with *there*, *two* with *to* and *too*

Don't say "*…being that…*"; say "*…because…*" or "*…since…*"

Don't use lower case *I* as a personal pronoun (text messaging is not acceptable!)

Numbers under 10 must be written out; 10 and above must be digits

Punctuation: comma usage, quotation marks, punctuation within quotation marks

Examples of slang terms to avoid: *okay, guy, cool, chill, 'till, 'cause, messed up, bunch, fun* (as an adjective)

Avoid dropped words: "*…couple hours…*" should be "*couple of hours…*", "*…over my friend's house…*" should be "*…over at my friend's house…*"

Learn the difference between word groups: *every day* and *everyday*, *all right* and *alright*

Capital, or upper-case, letters: Do not use capital letters for terms such as *high school* and *psychologist* unless you are referring to them by name/title.

I present these points of writing analysis to assist you in critiquing your own written presentations. Approach your writing and its style as a teacher might in looking at your work. Be aware of your strengths and weaknesses and deal with each appropriately, and your presentations will improve immensely.

- adapted from writeexpress.com, roanestate.edu, and Brookdale Community College Writing Criteria and Rubric

Working the Cause and Effect Process in Speaking and Writing

When you wish to present an idea, or series of ideas, which can lead to an expected, or even an unexpected, outcome, you need to base your written or spoken remarks on a cause and effect basis. Your emphasis should be on considering how events, situations, or decisions are connected by examining the start of a situation to a discussion of its results. You need to know the terminology involved before you begin: a **Cause** (or **Causes**) is an examination of *why* something has happened or exists, and an **Effect** (or **Effects**) is an examination of *what happens* as a result of an event, choice, decision, or situation.

To present an extremely effective piece, you need to select a topic that focuses on a problem that you have dealt with or faced because it has involved you directly. Personal involvement will make your presentation effective and relevant. Your presentation should focus on an important decision that you have had to make which sheds light upon the type of person you are and the way you think. As you prepare a topic for discussion, think of supporting points that will be based on personal experiences, observations, and opinions. This process should lead the reader or listener from the start of a situation to a discussion of its results.

Here's how to mentally compose a Cause and Effect point of view: it may be best to pose a question to yourself for your topic idea as this will help you get organized, then refine and use that question either as a title or refined further into a thesis comment. When you answer your question, the response(s) become(s) your thesis statement's developing idea(s). As you do this, think of your audience and ask yourself what aspects of this issue would interest them the most.

The difference between the Narration tool (discussed previously) and the Cause and Effect tool is in the type of details you select to use and how you organize these details. The focus and purpose of this style of presentation will be different, as well, as you will now need to <u>examine</u> something (perhaps a problem or a decision) through its causal and effectual points from which you will draw a conclusion about your topic and, ultimately, be teaching your reader something about you through your topic investigation. Remember that you need to interest your readers in what you are saying and get them to believe that your cause and effect idea is important to talk about. Therefore, it may be best to begin your essay with a personal story that shows what you are writing about so that the reader will clearly see the essay's topic and your personal connection to it.

Your organization of supporting details for your thesis is a crucial aspect of this type of presentation. The most logical way to show your ideas is by stating a key cause leading to a key effect, or effects (ex.: global warming may lead to animal species extinctions). Another structure which could be the most impactful would be to state your effect(s) at the outset and then trace back to causal points (ex.: people experience bankruptcy in many ways). You may also wish to present multiple effects from a series of causes (ex.: the interpretation of the impacts of various technologies on society is wide-ranging). Another scenario to consider is how two seemingly unrelated causes can lead to a singular effect (ex.: My mother came home very late one night from work and the electric company shut off our power as we paid our bill late, so we all had to eat cold beans and Rice Krispies for dinner). Strange ... but logical. Finally, there is the cause and effect "chain reaction" in which the effect of one cause may, in fact, be the cause of another effect, which could be yet another cause, and so on (Joe lunged at Billy but didn't hit him. Billy slipped to the floor, however, and badly hurt his arm. We had to call the EMT's who took him to the local hospital where his arm was set in a cast).

In creating the body of your essay, use your title to present your point of view, or use a cause question or an effect question as I mentioned earlier. Remember, there are probably many causes leading to the one major effect you want to highlight, or there could be many effects stemming from a single cause. You should brainstorm and mentally outline three to five reasons why a reader should accept your cause and effect thesis, and you will need to have ample support for your points as key pieces of evidence. Your evidence should be in the form of **examples, statistics, authorities (expert opinion), anecdotes, case histories, "hard" evidence, quotes,** and **scenarios.** Always feel that you are "reasoning" with your audience, so to make your reasons plausible, connect them back to your original position by using **"if ... then..."** logic. If you are speculating about a cause and/or effect, make your **"educated guesses"** seem believable through the evidence you provide.

Your conclusion should be a re-statement of your original premise, and, although your issue could be viewed in a different light, you must persuade your reader that your way of thinking about this issue is better. After presenting conclusions for your issue, tell why you reject other ideas and anticipate readers' objections or their preferred opinions by disputing them with accuracy and logic. A final statement about your point of view could be a prediction of an anticipated, or an unanticipated, outcome.

Before submitting the document, be aware of faulty logic and unclear organization. Use **climactic order** by mentioning minor causes first and then the most important cause or effect to conclude OR **descending order** by presenting the most important, or major, cause or effect first and then backtrack to more minor, but underlying, cause(s) or effect(s). Avoid spending too much time on obvious or predictable causes or effects by mentioning causes or effects expected and say why these are not the main, or major, points. Above all, avoid mistaking effects for causes and vice-versa.

- Adapted from www.hubpages.com, www. roanestate.edu, and www.brookdalecc.edu

CULTURAL AWARENESS

Being on Time: A Cultural Difference

In the United States, it is important to be on time, or punctual, for an appointment, a class, or a meeting. However, this may not be true in all countries. When you have business dealings abroad or with another nation, remember what happened to this particular person and adjust your approach accordingly.

An American professor discovered a cultural difference while teaching a class in a Brazilian university. The two-hour class was scheduled to begin at 10 a.m. and end at 12 p.m. On the first day when the professor arrived on time, no one was in the classroom. Many students came after 10 a.m., several arrived after 10:30 a.m., and two students came after 11 a.m. Although all the students greeted the professor as they arrived, few apologized for their lateness. Were these students being rude? He decided to study the students' behavior.

The professor talked to American and Brazilian students about lateness in both an informal and a formal situation: at lunch with a friend and in a university class, respectively. He gave the students to whom he spoke an example and asked them how they would react. If they had a lunch appointment with a friend, the average American student defined lateness as 19 minutes after the agreed time. On the other hand, the average Brazilian student felt the friend was late after 33 minutes.

In a United States university, students are expected to arrive at the appointed hour. In contrast, in Brazil neither the teacher nor the students always arrive at the appointed hour. Classes not only begin at the scheduled time in the United States, but they also end at the scheduled time. In the Brazilian class, only a few students left the class at noon; many remained past 12:30 to discuss the class and ask more questions. While arriving late may not be very important in Brazil, neither is staying late.

The explanation for these differences is complicated. People from Brazilian and North American cultures have different feelings about lateness. In Brazil, the students believe that a person who usually arrives late is probably more successful than a person who is always on time. In fact, Brazilians expect a person with status or prestige to arrive late. In the United States, however, lateness is usually considered to be disrespectful and unacceptable. Consequently, if a Brazilian is late for an appointment with a North American, the American may misinterpret the reason for the lateness and become angry.

As a result of this study, the professor learned that the Brazilian students were not being disrespectful to him. Instead, they were simply behaving in the appropriate way for Brazilian students in Brazil. Eventually, the professor was able to adapt his own behavior so that he could feel comfortable in the new culture.

Neither the professor nor the students were wrong. As you interact with those of another culture, be cognizant of certain kinds of differences and distinction to be made. Understanding the process another individual is working with in a business venture will greatly enhance the product you wish to obtain. Research will go a long way to assist you in this regard.

My Experience with Culture Shock

I served for two years as one of the earliest Peace Corps Volunteers (1962 – 1964) in the southern Philippine Islands on the island of Jolo where they had not seen a person from the Western Hemisphere, other than missionaries, since their liberation from the Japanese by American forces in 1946. My housemate, Jack, who was a classmate of mine at the University of Notre Dame and persuaded me to accompany him to a session on campus with a Peace Corps recruiter, was an integral part of the following episode, and I thank him often for indirectly saving my life.

My story seems funny now in retrospect, but at the time it was shocking, almost deadly. The southern area of The Philippines is almost 95% Indonesian Muslim, even though the majority of the country is 95% Catholic. Our little island in the South Seas is actually closer to the mainland of Indonesia, with the largest Muslim population in the world, than it is to the Philippines' larger islands to the north. Many of the customs and religious observances we experienced were new to us, and no one who trained us for our two-year mission knew of the uniqueness of our situation. We had no electricity or running water for our two years, and we were trained to be teachers and community developers, but we had little or no knowledge of the language or the uniqueness of this part of the world. We had been in the country for only four months and were just beginning to get acclimated to our surroundings and our jobs.

On one particular night, near the conclusion of the Month of Ramadan, one of the holiest months in the Muslim calendar, Jack and I had just received an invitation to the house of Mayor Lincoln Tulawie as his seventh wife had just given birth to a baby girl and asked us to come by and see her and have light refreshments. He would have invited us for a full dinner, but during Ramadan, a Muslim must fast from sunrise to sunset and then eat only sparingly otherwise. We were thrilled at this invitation as another one of his wives was the Principal of Bilaan Elementary School where we worked. His house was about two miles down the only road in our barrio of Bilaan, and between our house and his was a military compound manned by the Philippine Constabulary (PC), the local law enforcement group in the area. Interestingly, all PC personnel were Catholic, from northern islands, as it was appropriate then to have non-Muslims in control of the Muslim populace, saving much "bad blood."

Regarding the month of Ramadan, because of fasting and deep devotional periods of each day, many people of the local sect of Islamic faith were extremely frazzled and high-strung at that time. Some of the more zealous devotees actually hallucinated, with the assistance of local drugs, and acted strangely. We later learned that, during Ramadan, if any male member of this sect had a dream in which he saw a white horse riding in the sky, it was a sign to him that the Islamic god, Allah, was summoning him to heaven, and the only way he could achieve "nirvana" was to kill as many non-believers as he could before he, in turn, was killed: it was a kind of ritualized suicide. This action was called "running amok" which is a term we still use today for someone's activities which are odd, weird, and dangerous. Making matters more unusual for the "dreamer," is that he could run amok only on the evening of a full moon and use only a machete as his murder weapon. Furthermore, if a particular male had that dream, all other male members of that person's family had to run amok alongside the "dreamer."

Jack and I began to prepare for our trek to Mayor Tulawie's house, but we were running late as Jack, who had lost over twenty pounds because he could not get used to the exotic food we had to eat, could not find a pair of pants that would fit him. We had heard from our neighbors about the amok tradition, but we had not experienced any incident within the month, so we were preparing to visit the Mayor that particular evening without a second thought, as we were so pleased at being invited. Finally, I gave Jack a pair of my pants, and we were set to leave the house. We walked down the few steps from our entranceway to the road and began walking when we heard a series of rifle shots and heard bullets slicing through the banana leaves over our heads. Jack and I dove into the roadside ditch and lay there without moving or talking for many long minutes. Finally, Jack mentioned to me that we could probably go on our way safely, but I said that idea was foolish at this point, and we should get right back home. As we got back inside, more shots rang out, and we then grabbed our two single mattresses, as we were told to do during an amok, and propped them up against our front door for protection while we crouched down behind them, and waited.

The next day many people were out and about, and we slowly began to hear the story of what had transpired. It seems that one Islamic male of this sect had experience the "dream," and he and two other male members of his family, one being a twelve-year boy, had run amok. They decided to infiltrate the PC camp grounds, as, of course, that's where the so-called non-believers were headquartered. That night, after moonrise, each of them broke through the chicken wire surrounding the camp and advanced toward the barracks. The commanding officer, who knew of the Ramadan tradition well, slept with a pistol under his pillow, but his window was left open, and the eldest male jumped through it. At the last second, the officer grabbed his pistol and shot his attacker. The next oldest male was also shot near another barrack, but the young boy lost his nerve and ran from the PC camp down the road toward our house. It was he whom the PC were shooting at in pursuit as he ran past us. To a member of this sect, coming out of an amok attack alive is almost worse than death as he is shunned by his family and his community, totally ostracized.

Here's where Jack saved my life; if he had found a pair of pants that fit him, he and I, on our trip to the Mayor's, would have been right in front of the PC camp when the shooting started! Timing is everything in life…

Days later, after apologies to the Mayor who totally understood our situation, we were invited again to his house, this time after the conclusion of Ramadan, for a local feast, which we found out was to be a banquet in our honor. Even though the Mayor was not wealthy, he spared no expense and had gone all out to prepare this feast for the Americans. We sat along a large rectangular table and were, at first, served a bowl of hot broth soup, and because there were no utensils, we lifted the bowl to our lips and drank the liquid. After the soup bowls were cleared away, I remarked to the Mayor, in my broken dialect, how the clear both was so tasty and how succulent the olive in the soup was. He looked at me in a funny way and said, "That was no olive. That was the eyeball of a sheep!" I probably then turned many shades of green and wondered what our next course would be. We were then served a fruit salad which was laid out on a large banana leaf for each diner. Since there were no utensils, we knew, from earlier experiences, to use the thumb and two forefingers of our left hand to eat – the left hand only, as the right hand was known as the "impure hand," since it was used for wiping in the outhouse. I must have been the first person finished with this course and, thinking that the banana leaf was a part of the "salad," I proceeded to pick up the leaf and started chewing on it. As each of the others at the table finished the salad, they, too, picked up their banana leaf and started to chew on it. It wasn't until after the meal was over that one of the braver of the guests told me that I had eaten the "plate." Yet, in a gracious fashion typical of Asian countries, each guest began to devour the leaf so that I, the outsider, would "save face!"

www.ingramcontent.com/pod-product-compliance
Lightning Source LLC
Chambersburg PA
CBHW021500210526
45463CB00002B/826